Investments and CyberWorld: 2 Book Boxed Set for Beginners

By

Alex Nkenchor Uwajeh

This collection includes:

*Money: Small Business Opportunities - Money Making Ideas - Start Your Own Business for Beginners - Escape the Rat Race and Be Your Own Boss.

*Finance: Cloud Computing, Cyber Security and Cyber Heist - Beginners Guide to Help Protect Against Online Theft in the Cyber World.

Book One

Money: Small Business Opportunities - Money Making Ideas - Start Your Own Business for Beginners - Escape the Rat Race and Be Your Own Boss.

Introduction

Deciding to start a business can be one of the most exciting decisions you'll make in your lifetime. Being your own boss can be an extremely fulfilling experience, both professionally and personally.

However, there's also plenty of work involved in creating a successful business enterprise.

Fortunately, there are some types of businesses that can be established relatively easily and without a big investment to get you started. If you set up your business plan right in the beginning, it's also possible to build your business into a million dollar empire.

The key is to find a business and an industry that you are passionate about, and then test the waters on a part-time basis. Some of the world's most successful businesses began as part-time ideas in someone's living room or basement or garage that grew into major corporations over time.

Throughout this book, we'll also look at some million-dollar-business case studies that began as small operations and grew into large corporations.

Are you ready to look into some business ideas?

Party Services

Everybody wants their parties to be memorable, but they often don't have the time or the ability to organize everything that needs to be done to create such an event. Of course, they also want a way to memorialize the event too so they can look back on it some day and remember fun times.

Offering party services allows others to spend more time socializing and enjoying the event without the stress of planning, organizing, cooking, serving, taking photos or videos, or otherwise trying to find activities or entertainment to help keep the party going.

Party Planning Services

As a party planner, your job is to create some of the most memorable moments in people's lives. A party planner organizes a particular party, gathering, or event in line with the customer's preferences.

As your own boss, you have the option of offering to plan all types of parties, or you can choose to specialize in specific types of parties that you enjoy the most. **Some options open to you include:**

Anniversary party

Baby showers

Birthday parties

Children's parties

Cocktail or dinner parties

Corporate parties and functions

Engagement parties

Family reunions

Retirement parties

Themed parties and events

Wedding showers and wedding receptions

You can choose to offer full service party planning, where you arrange and handle every detail of the party, right from décor and decorations, to activities and entertainment, through to catering and service for food and drink. Most planners who offer full service also attend the party to ensure everything runs smoothly.

Alternatively, you might want to specialize in just certain aspects of the party, such as arranging catering, or refreshments and beverages, or just the décor and decorations, or just venue location.

Before you get started, you'll need to look into what licenses some state and local governments require. You may also want to invest in liability insurance to protect you in the event that a guest is injured or causes damage to the party venue.

You'll also need to spend some time putting together a list of potential new business contacts to help you supply your parties. For example, you'll need access to a list of reliable local caterers, photographers, suppliers, and entertainers, along with access to a range of different venue options.

Cleaning services

Cleaning services are always in demand. If it can get dirty, there is someone out there willing to pay you to clean it. In fact, professional cleaning is one of the few industries with such a wide variety of opportunities to start your own business for a small cost outlay.

Home Cleaning

Starting a residential cleaning service is a highly effective way to start a business that can be run on a full-time or part-time basis from home.

The majority of home cleaning businesses offer maid services. You'll be cleaning, dusting, sweeping, mopping, vacuuming, and scrubbing other people's homes.

Many people start out offering their services to friends, neighbors, or family members. If you do a good job in their homes, some of them are likely to recommend your services to other people, which is a great way to increase your customer base.

Alternatively, you can put flyers into neighborhood mailboxes advertising your services in your local area.

You'll need to transport your own cleaning materials to each job, including a broom, a mop, cleaning products, sponges, and a squeegee. Some customers may let you use their regular household vacuum cleaner. Others may request that you bring one instead.

Commercial Cleaning

If you're willing to work at times when others don't, you could start a commercial cleaning service. Many business owners will happily pay someone to come in and clean their offices or stores after normal working hours.

Some commercial businesses may need you to provide basic janitorial services, such as mopping and polishing floors, vacuuming, emptying garbage bins, and cleaning staff kitchen and toilet facilities.

You will need some tools to complete your job, including a commercial-grade vacuum cleaner, a floor buffer, rubber gloves, a mop, bucket, sponges, a squeegee, garbage bags, and cleaning products.

You can hand out your business card or your flyer advertising your services to local businesses, or send out your flyer in a direct mail campaign to gain new customers.

Carpet Cleaning

It's common for people to put off until later any chore that needs special equipment. Carpet cleaning is one of those tasks. Homeowners know the importance of maintaining their carpets, but many are afraid to use the rented do-it-yourself carpet shampoo machines or steam cleaning machines for fear of damaging them.

You will need to buy some equipment before you get started. You'll need a carpet extraction machine, a carpet cleaning wand with at least two jets, jet upholstery tool, a stair cleaning tool, a slow speed scrubber, carpet grooming rake, corner guards, carpet pre-spray solution, and acid rinse conditioner. You'll also need to take out general liability insurance for your business.

Window Cleaning

Window cleaning is an excellent business for anyone on a shoestring budget. You can get started with only a small cash outlay and be in business almost immediately.

You will need a bucket, sponge, window scrubber, squeegee, and window cleaning soap. If your customers have two-story homes or offices you might also need an extension pole for your scrubber and squeegee, or a ladder.

Residential customers may not always be regular about booking your services, but they can form a healthy part of your overall income.

By comparison, commercial customers are far more likely to book your services on a regular basis. Owners of offices, restaurants, or retail stores like to keep their businesses looking clean and fresh, so approach local businesses and let them know about your services.

Gardening and Lawn Care

Lawn and garden care services are always popular. After all, homeowners want their homes to look good, but they don't always have the time to get out and look after the lawns or garden beds.

Your job will be to mow, edge, trim, and fertilize lawns for around 20 to 30 clients each week. Some clients may also ask you to maintain garden beds by pulling weeds, pruning bushes and trees, or just keeping the garden looking neat and tidy.

You'll need a well-maintained lawn mower, a lawn edger, leaf blower, and a rake. You may also need a truck or trailer to transport your tools and equipment to each customer's home, along with offering the option of removing grass clippings for those customers who want this service.

Lawn care is a seasonal business, with some downtime during late fall and winter for around two-thirds of the country. Prime lawn growing months are usually from April to early October.

As the grass-growing season is limited to certain times throughout the year, you have the option of working longer hours during spring and summer to build up your income and your customer base.

If you're careful about marketing your services aggressively enough throughout the lawn care season, you should be able to put aside enough funds to carry you through the income-free winter months.

Alternatively, you could expand your services to include other seasonal activities. You could offer existing clients gutter cleaning services through fall and snowplowing or snow shoveling services through winter if you're keen to continue working.

You should find that clients who are already happy with your lawn care services throughout the rest of the year will see the benefit in continuing to hire you for other services through down times too.

Gutter Cleaning

Most people dread cleaning their home gutters, but it is an essential chore that must be done regularly. If you're willing to do the job, there's plenty of business out there and demand is always high.

Cleaning gutters involves removing any debris that has built up in the rain gutters of residential homes. The gunk that builds up in gutters can stain anything it touches, so you'll need to remove it from the gutter using a scoop or your hands and place it into a bucket to be disposed of once you're on the ground again.

Your biggest expenses when starting a gutter cleaning business will be ladders. You'll also need to invest in good safety ropes, a harness, and a lanyard to protect yourself against falling. It's also a good idea to consider protecting yourself with insurance, as you'll be working on ladders and rooftops.

The rest of your equipment and tools are easy. You'll need heavy rubber gloves, gutter scoop, heavy garbage bags, and a 5-gallon bucket.

Distribute flyers to homes in your local area at least a month before gutter cleaning season begins. Neighborhoods with lots of large, leafy trees near homes are ideal.

Keep in mind that gutter cleaning is a seasonal business, so you'll only be working through some periods of the year. In many parts of the country, autumn is gutter-cleaning time.

However, as the demand for gutter cleaning is so high, you have the potential to earn a substantial amount of money over a short period of time. If you have a lawn care business that slows down in the fall, gutter cleaning is a great way to supplement your income.

Snow Removal Services

Snow removal services are definitely a seasonal business, but there is the potential to earn a substantial income in a short period of time. Your job is to remove built up snow from sidewalks, driveways, and pathways to a customer's home so they don't have to. It's common to hear of snowplow operators earning $1,000 per day when the snow is blowing.

You can attach a snow blade to your mower or your truck and offer snowplowing services. For snow and ice removal services, you'll also need a shovel, a salt spreader for de-icing, and a self-propelled snow blower.

Start advertising your snow removal services to existing customers and other people within the local at least a month before winter sets in. If you already have a lawn care service, this is a great option to supplement your income through the winter months.

Of course, if you pick up new customers through winter, chances are they'll continue to book you for your other services through the spring, summer, and fall months too.

Car Cleaning and Auto Detailing Services

Car cleaning and auto detailing services are in high demand. Anyone with a car who wants to keep it looking good and has the income to pay for your services is a potential customer.

Your job is to wash, and wax other people's cars. You'll be vacuuming and shampooing carpets, cleaning upholstery, polishing chrome and cleaning tires.

The big advantages of having a car cleaning business are that you can start it on a shoestring budget and you can choose to run it part-time, if that suits your schedule.

Your equipment will include a wet/dry vacuum, a mini-carpet shampooer, a buffer or polisher, brushes, sponges, buckets, soap, window cleaner, and wax. You'll also need a vehicle to cart all your tools around in.

You will need to know which car cleaning products are safe for what types of finishes and which ones produce the best results. It's also fairly intensive labor, so you'll need to be fit and healthy enough to keep at it.

Ironing / Mobile Laundry Service

Let's face it: busy people will pay you to do the tasks they're too busy to complete. If you're willing to offer ironing or mobile laundry services to busy people, they'll pay your fee for the convenience of getting it done.

Most people dread the idea of ironing, but it's an essential part of life, so they'll figure that it's better to pay someone else to do it than to do it themselves.

You'll need the tools of your trade in order before you begin your business. At the very least, you'll need an iron and an ironing board. Once you expand your business operations, an ironing steam generator would be a good investment, as you can complete more items in a faster time frame.

A water descaler is also a good idea if you're using your iron for more than just regular home usage. It's worth the investment to stop your iron or steam generator from breaking down when you need it most.

Marketing your services should be relatively easy. You can start with flyers delivered to local homes within your neighborhood. You can also let word of mouth spread knowledge of your home business enterprise to gain new customers.

Work out your pricing and set a schedule of fees for the type of clothing items you're willing to iron. It's also a good idea to create some simple business policies about the types of clothing you won't accept for your business.

If possible, try to avoid charging by the hour for ironing services, as most people simply assume you'll take your time completing their chores. Set a price per item for your services so people can estimate their costs before they engage your services.

Food Businesses

If you've had countless compliments on your cupcakes, or you have people begging you to tell them your secret recipes for their favorite dishes, you might be able to turn your skills into a profitable business.

Starting a restaurant to showcase your culinary skills is expensive, but there are some more affordable options that offer an excellent way to launch a new food business idea.

No matter what food business you decide to start, you do need to obtain the necessary licenses and permits you'll need in order to sell food. Each state has their own individual permits and licensing requirements, so take some time to check what needs to be done.

You may also need to obtain permits to park your cart or truck on streets, near arenas or stadiums, at college campuses, in the business district, in a park or a mall, or on a beach property.

Food Kiosks and Carts

Food carts have been around for decades, but modern day carts have really cleaned up the image of street-food vendors. It's common to see foods such as hot-dogs, kebobs, or ice creams sold from carts, although there are plenty of other types of food carts around as well.

Food kiosks are often temporary stands or mobile booths designed for selling food. It's common to find pop-up food kiosks in flea markets, malls, movie theaters or stadiums.

Food carts are easy to maintain and much cheaper to get started, as compared to a food truck. There is also less licensing to worry about with a food cart than there is with other types of food trucks.

The highly mobile nature of a food cart means you can shift location to suit your customer base, or move around to suit weather conditions. Owning a food cart gives you the freedom to expand your customer base in new locations too. You can cash in on big events by temporarily placing your food cart near a stadium or conference center.

You will still need to obtain the necessary permits before you start trading. In some locations, you may also have to pay for rent on the street, in the mall, or at an event.

Food Truck Business

According to research conducted in Los Angeles, the street-food business is a $1 billion industry. The study included mobile food trucks, food carts, trailers, and kiosks that have popped up all over the country.

Food trucks have much lower start-up costs and operating overheads than running a brick-and-mortar restaurant, but a well-equipped food truck is considerably more expensive than a cart or kiosk.

Most food trucks do great business in corporate parks and other places with limited access to restaurants. If one location isn't generating enough income, you have the ability to move to a new location with better prospects.

Food trucks that offer specialty food and gourmet dishes also do very well in some areas. Specialty trucks usually focus on serving food not typically found in traditional food trucks.

Gourmet Snack Food

Packaging and selling your own homemade soup, jam, candy, salsa, or popcorn is easier than ever in recent times. Customers are always willing to try your new taste sensation and there are plenty of outlets available to start building up your customer base.

Of course, there is a range of health regulations, state laws, and rules you'll need to abide by if you hope to be successful. You may also be visited at random by health inspectors to ensure the food you're preparing, handling, and packaging is safe for your customers to consume. They also check that your manufacturing facilities are clean and meet stringent regulations.

Surprisingly, starting your own gourmet snack food business is relatively cost effective. You can begin operations right from your own kitchen bench. Until recently, many states banned the sale of any food made in a home kitchen.

You will need to be very careful about the ingredients you're able to use in your food products. You'll also need to be vigilant about your labeling, the types of foods you can sell, and where products can be sold.

For example, the US Department of Agriculture (USDA) has strict rules about food labels. You must list all the ingredients used in the manufacture of the product and the nutritional content, including calories, fat, cholesterol, proteins, and vitamins.

As your snack food enterprise grows, you also have the option of renting commercial kitchen premises.

While some entrepreneurs may happily approach retail outlets and chains to stock their products while they're still small, others may find that testing the market response works better for them.

Setting up a small food stall or kiosk at a flea market or farmer's market is a great way to test market response to your products before you spend too much money on creating huge batches of product. You'll also be earning some money back into the business while you develop your product lines.

There's also the advantage of getting your product out in front of people who have the potential of turning into loyal customers over the long term.

Once you're sure that the market is favorable to your products, go ahead and approach stores, chains, and other distributors to sell your homemade gourmet snack food products on their shelves for you.

Mobile Catering Service

Offering a mobile catering service allows you to take your business directly to your customers. Most catering services transport the food to the event that are usually served on trays or buffet style.

The advantage of a mobile catering service over a food truck is that you don't risk as much in inventory as you're only cooking and bringing food to cater for the number of people at the party or event.

You also have the advantage of not having to worry if a particular destination will be busy or not, as you already know how many people will be at your destination.

Million Dollar Case Study #1

Janine Allis had a dream of providing healthy juice and smoothies to customers. She began her business enterprise on her kitchen bench.

When she was ready to take the leap, her fruit juices and smoothies were first sold in a small food kiosk located in Adelaide, South Australia in 2000. The entrepreneur worked hard to ensure her little store thrived, building it into a profitable enterprise.

Since that time, her little juice business has expanded to include more than 350 Boost Juice franchises in more than 15 countries around the world, from Australia, to Portugal, Russia, Singapore, India, Chile, Germany, Dubai, and the United Kingdom.

Franchising agreements for the juice bar have also been secured in Mexico, China and Thailand.

Million Dollar Case Study #2

Angie Bastian was a mother of two who hoped to earn a little bit of extra cash part-time to put into her kids' college funds, but her little idea expanded into a $50 million business.

Angie grew up eating popcorn done created by her mother as a weekend tradition. She wanted to bring some of their favorite flavor combinations to other people, so she bought some kettle corn equipment and experimented with different flavors until she landed on some winners.

When she had her special recipe just right, she convinced a storeowner to allow her to set up a small food stall outside a grocery store. Within the first three hours her little stall made $300.

She expanded operations to set up her stall outside amateur baseball games in the evenings and out from of the local Home Depot store on weekends.

Before long, the Minnesota Vikings were asking if Angie's Popcorn could become the official popcorn snack for the team. Everyone wanted to know where they could buy it.

At that point, Angie and her family went from being food stall vendors to manufacturers of the massively popular Angie's Popcorn brand. They added 50 kettles to their modest little operation and expanded to hire 150 employees. By that point, the Angie's Popcorn brand was being sold on the shelves at Costco and Target.

Pet Businesses

Many pet owners treat their pets just like their children. They want the best care options, the best food options, and the best lifestyle they can provide for their beloved pets.

Providing products or services for pets is a growing industry. After all, Americans spend more than $30 billion annually on their pets.

If you love animals and you want to create a business that revolves around pets, you have a huge number of options available to you.

Pet Sitting

There are many pet owners who can't leave a pet at a boarding kennel or with friends or family. The pet may have a chronic health condition, or it may be an exotic pet that is difficult to take care of.

Then there are people who prefer to keep their pet in a familiar, safe environment, rather than sending them to an unfamiliar boarding facility, so they'll hire a pet sitter to be at home when they're not.

Some people also hire pet sitters for short periods of time, such as a night out, or a day off. No matter what your customers' reasons are, there is definitely a market for good pet sitting services.

You can market your pet sitting services through other pet-related businesses in your area. For example, vets, dog grooming salons, dog training centers or local pet stores.

Dog Day Care

Dog day care facilities are incredibly popular with owners who don't want to leave their dogs at home alone while they're at work. Dogs are highly social creatures and need contact and interaction throughout the day.

A dog day care center is designed for owners to drop off their pet in the morning and pick them up again in the evening. It's not intended to be a long-term boarding kennel, so there are no overnight stays.

If you have sufficient space and a securely enclosed yard, you can start your business at home.

However, a better alternative is to rent a warehouse that has a securely fenced outdoor space and convert it into a day care facility. You can provide comfortable indoor areas for dogs, including lounges and beds, play areas inside and outside with dog-safe toys, or even add water features.

Install some web-cams around the indoor and outdoor areas and connect them to a private area of your website. Owners who want to check what their dogs are doing through the day can log in and view footage of their dogs playing or sleeping or just doing what dogs do.

Pet Photography

If you're good with photography, what better way to earn a living than by photographing people's beloved pets? You can operate on a mobile basis, or from a home-based studio, or from pet shops, or a combination of all three.

Owners want to create precious memories of their pets, so make your photography service fun and interesting by offering themed backdrops, costumes, or other ways to ensure your customers look amazing in each photo you take.

You also have the option of boosting your profits by offering other products that allow customer to transfer their pet photos onto. For example, you can offer calendars, greeting cards, t-shirts, or mugs to customers that have their pets' photos transferred onto.

Gourmet Pet Treats

The fastest growing area in the pet food industry is gourmet dog treats. People love their dogs and they want the very best dog treats they can find.

Most pet owners are aware that commercially bought treats and pet foods often contain preservatives, artificial colorings and flavorings, and other fillers. In an effort to ensure their pets are eating a healthy diet, owners seek out pet treats containing natural ingredients.

Creating your dog treats at home is relatively easy. You'll need some recipes, some molds to create cute shapes, and some packaging materials.You will need to check that any recipes you use contain ingredients that aren't harmful to dogs, as their digestive systems are different to ours.

A great way to diversify your product lines is to cater to dogs that have food intolerances. For example, some dogs are gluten-intolerant so create gluten-free options.

You can market your products at local flea markets, pet stores and retailers, veterinary clinics, dog grooming salons, at pet fairs, or directly through an online storefront.

Buy a Business

Not everyone is keen on the idea of building a brand new business from the ground up. A new business means finding new customers to get the business rolling, sorting out business plans and operations models, and marketing your services to customers who may prefer to buy from established brands rather than from a start-up.

By comparison, if you have the funding to do so, you can buy an existing business or purchase the franchising license for a well-established brand.

Turnkey Business

A turnkey business is one that is already established and operating. There are plenty of advantages of buying a turnkey business, but there are also a few disadvantages to consider.

Before you take the leap into buying a business that is already established, take a moment to consider the pros and cons.

Advantages

Most people automatically assume that buying an established business is less risky than starting a new business. You're able to view the financial history of the business and take over existing operations, so there should be very little disruption in normal business. The primary advantages of buying a turnkey business are:

Less risk associated with an established business than beginning a new start-up

Business plans and procedures are already in place

Immediate cash flow from continued operations

Financial history already in place

Existing customer base and contacts with suppliers, staff, equipment, and stock

An established market for the product or services

Existing employees can continue daily operations as required

Disadvantages

Not every business for sale on the market is a good investment. Many business owners may be selling out of the business because the market may be unsteady. The industry may be on the decline, or the business may be under-performing. Many people believe that a struggling business being sold cheaply could represent a real bargain and an opportunity to build it back up to its real potential. However, there are some disadvantages to consider before buying a turnkey business, including:

Larger initial investment to get started as compared to starting a business from scratch

The existing business may need major financial contributions to update or replace old plan and equipment

The business may be operating in a poor location

The previous business owners may have developed a poor business reputation with past customers

There may be bad managers or employees already within the business

The business could be within a declining industry niche, which negatively affects future growth and expansion.

Before investing into any business enterprise, it's vitally important to conduct your due diligence.

Franchise Business

Buying a franchise business means you have a well-known brand that operates under exactly the same business procedures as every other franchise outlet, so customers know what they're getting with your products or services.

However, there are always advantages and disadvantages to every business opportunity. Before you jump into a franchise business, consider some of the pros and cons. You should also note that not all franchise opportunities will include or incorporate the factors listed below.

Advantages

Having access to an established way of doing business that replicates a certain customer experience is a definite bonus. After all, you can walk into any McDonalds store in Thailand or Australia and receive the same products and service as you'd get right here at home. **Some of the biggest advantages to buying a franchise system include:**

Well-established brand, product, or service

Full assistance from the franchisor with site selection, lease negotiation, site development, and shop fitters

Assistance with finance options or securing finance from banks or other lenders

Initial management training

Ongoing management assistance

Established standard business procedures, operating manuals, and stock control systems

Established financial systems already in place

Franchisor deals with marketing and advertising for the business

Disadvantages

Of course, while a franchise system sounds like an easy way to get started in business, there are always downsides to consider. Some of the biggest disadvantages include:

Restricted territory in which you can operate or promote your business

Ongoing payment of fees to the franchisor

The franchisor is not obliged to renew your franchise agreement at the end of the franchise term

Less autonomy in business decisions or addition of new product lines

Selling your business may mean paying fees to the franchisor, reducing any profits you may have built up

Restrictions on the sale or termination of the franchise

Home Care Services

More people are realizing the benefits of providing care services from home. There are plenty of people out there who prefer the personalized touch. Home care services are also sometimes more affordable options than professional care services.

Here are some options you might consider:

Senior Care Services

Providing non-medical senior care services is a growing industry. After all, there are a lot of aging baby boomers out there that need non-medical assistance from day to day.

Some may require a responsible driver to provide transportation to attend appointments or to get the week's grocery shopping done. Some may want some assistance with meal preparation, handling, and cooking.

There are also seniors out there who will happily pay for concierge services, where you help run errands, deal with basic cleaning services, help with grooming and basic dressing needs, or help out with computer training or support.

Others may simply pay for a level of companion care, where you'll spend time with your clients completing puzzles, playing games, accompanying the person to fitness classes or taking a walk together to ensure the person's safety during exercise, or just providing important social interaction they otherwise wouldn't receive.

Of course, you can choose to run your business as the organizer and administrator while you oversee a staff of medically-trained professionals who provide more in-depth medication management, wound dressing and care, and other related types of care.

While many seniors will be lucid and active, there will be some that will suffer from infirmities and varying degrees of mental capacity.

Your job is to become a huge asset to your aging clients. You can do this by providing your own services. You can also help by providing information about various services that can make their lives easier.

Home-Based Daycare business

Home-based day care services are a great option for those people who have the time and energy to look after other people's kids. As a business owner, you can set your own hours based on your preferences.

The best part about running a home-based day care business is that you get to stay at home with your own kids while earning money. In most states, a home-based day care business can accept up to six children at one time, with no more than two children under the age of 2.

Starting your day care business doesn't require a large initial investment. However, if you're living in a rental property you may need to get permission from your landlord to operate a business from home.

Space Requirements

You will need to check that your home has the minimum number of square feet of space per child in care according to your state's laws. Most states require a minimum of 35 square feet per child, as well as having a safe outdoor space for play areas. You can find out the requirements in your state by contacting the agency that deals with day care licensing in your area.

Activities and Care Options

Keep in mind that providing family day care services is much more than just babysitting other people's kids. You'll be required to provide play areas, fun activities to keep kids entertained, educational activities, quiet space for nap time, and meals.

If your service accepts very young children, you'll also be responsible for changing diapers and potty training.

Insurance

Your business will need to take out additional insurance to cover your home day care business. Some states may ask you to have CPR and first-aid certificates before you start accepting children. Other states may also require that you complete courses in child development, child abuse prevention, nutrition, and other health-related courses.

Business Policy and Contracts

Before you open for business, it's important to spend some time planning and organizing how you'll operate your business. Each child you accept into your home for day care services will need to have a contract signed by the parents.

Your contract needs to include your business policies for payment, fees for any late payments or bounced checks, and charges for vacations, paid holidays and overtime.

Other things to include in your contract policies include sick children, scheduling and discipline rules. If you're not sure how to get started with your policies, contact your local home child-care licensing agency and ask for a sample contract.

Flea Market Entrepreneur

Thinking about creating a retail business, but don't have the cash to get started? Why not consider your local flea market or swap meet as a cheap entry point into the market?

Flea markets provide the ideal environment to incubate a business idea. Art shows, craft fairs, flea markets, or farmers markets are excellent venues for growing and expanding a business idea or a hobby into a profitable retail business.

Most street fairs and markets have a very low entry cost. All you'll need is transport, a table, a cash box, your produces, and the fee to cover the cost of renting a small booth. Some states may also require you have a vendor's license, but the majority of flea markets provide vendors with plenty of information to help you get started.

Flea markets and swap meets are an excellent way to test the market for new business ideas. Vendors who set up at flea markets can gauge the market response for new products and check how various products fare with customer interest levels.

Many people who enjoy crafts and handmade goods do well at flea markets, as they're able to make their own products. However, they're sometimes limited to selling only as much as they can make.

Other vendors do very well buying products from wholesalers and selling them at retail prices directly to customers. The food and beverage side of the flea market business is also a highly profitable way to test new business ideas.

It's up to you whether you only want to operate on weekends on a part-time basis, or whether you aim at offering your products to a broader audience at daily swap meets.

Being at flea markets on a regular basis gives you the opportunity to be face-to-face with your customers. You have the opportunity to learn what they like about your business, what could be improved and what they would like to buy if you sold other items.

Having a regular presence at a local flea market also means building up a loyal customer base. Most vendors have websites to showcase their products, along with online storefronts, and maintain a healthy online presence with customers following on various social media sites.

You also have a brilliant opportunity to learn from other vendors. More experienced vendors will often have tips and advice for newer people at the markets.

You can choose to stick to local flea markets as you build your business, or move around to other swap meets and markets in nearby areas to expand your customer base. You can also choose to offer your products for sale via an online storefront to help increase sales.

Perhaps the best part of operating a flea market business is having the opportunity to see whether your business idea will work for your goals. If standing behind a table at a flea market isn't your dream job, use your time to build your customers, grow your product lines, and aim at opening a store when sales get big enough.

Million Dollar Business Case Study #3

It's surprising how many people underestimate the power of flea markets. Yet they remain a highly profitable way to start and test the strength of any retail business.

Back in 1998, Jack and Marilou Johar opened a small stall at the Paramount Swap Meet in California. They purchased good quality leather products from wholesalers and displayed them at various swap meets.

On their first day of business they sold $500 of product. Before long they expanded to a larger, permanent stall space at a daily swap meet in Anaheim, California.

By 2001, the couple were grossing around $10,000 per month in sales.

As the business grew, they tested new product lines in their swap meet stall and expanded their product line accordingly.

By 2005, the little flea market operation had grown into the Street Leathers Corp and moved into a wholesale warehouse space in Los Angeles that generates around $2.5 million in sales each year.

Crafting and Homemade Products

Do you have some skill at creating homemade crafted goods? There is a huge market out there for these types of items.

People love to buy homemade items, from blankets to sweaters to cute knitted toys, as they simply don't have the time to create these things themselves.

The benefit of creating a business around crafting ideas is that you can broaden your clientele with multiple online outlets, as well as selling as local flea markets, farmer's markets, and craft fairs. People like to know that the items they're buying are hand-made by the designer or crafter, as it adds a touch of authenticity and uniqueness to the product.

There is a vast range of homemade products you can sell to make huge profits from home. **Here are just some of them:**

Knitting / Crocheting

If you enjoy knitting or crocheting, there are so many opportunities available for you to earn money. People love hand-made knitted or crocheted items and they're willing to pay a premium for you to make them.

Most people associate knitting with ugly Christmas sweaters and associate crochet with granny squares and lap blankets. However, modern patterns allow for knitting and crochet designs to create cute plushie toys, blankets, clothing, homeware items, accessories, and a range of other items that are limited only by your imagination.

The problem with creating your business around only what you can make is that you're limited to the number of items you can create in a specified time frame.

Knitting and crocheting are both hobbies that take time and effort. If you're happy with the idea of earning a comfortable part-time income while you're watching TV in the evening, then it's a great option for you.

However, if you're keen to turn your hobby into a full-time enterprise, you may need to be a little more creative about ways to generate income.

For example, there are talented people out there who love to knit and crochet. They produce gorgeous items from their hobby that they sell for healthy profits. What those people may not realize is that they can also sell clearly-worded patterns for new designs to other crafters so they can make the same items themselves.

Websites like Etsy.com, craftsy.com, and ravelry.com feature knitted and crocheted patterns that other crafters can purchase so they can do it themselves.

The small amount of money most designers charge to buy patterns seems unreasonable, especially considering the amount of work that goes into creating each pattern. However, if you consider multiple knitters and crocheters are always looking for new projects to work on, the sheer volume of sales could easily drive your income through the roof.

Sewing and Quilting Services

A home sewing business is a great way to earn some extra income from your sewing skills. If you're handy with simple clothing alterations or repairs, there are plenty of people out there who will want to take advantage of your services.

Of course, if you have a talent for dressmaking, you can advertise your services for creating made-to-order wedding dresses, bridal outfits, bridesmaid dresses, or even prom dresses. There's also the option of creating unique quilts, cushions, and other soft furnishings that are always in demand.

If you're creative, you can even make cute plush toys or matched kid's clothing sets. Build up some stock of your toys or clothing items and head down to the local craft fair to sell your products. You have the opportunity of advertising your primary dressmaking services at the same time as attracting new customers to your services.

You will need a robust sewing machine and an overlocking machine to get started. Promote your services on Etsy.com, using completed garments to show styles and then let customers know you'll take custom orders for people who want a garment in the same style.

Soap Making

Homemade soap-making businesses have the potential to grow into very profitable enterprises. People are becoming more concerned about the number of chemicals, artificial colors and fragrances, and synthetic ingredients in beauty products. There are also people out there with sensitive skin and allergies who often find it difficult to buy soap that won't irritate their skin.

Both of these things mean there's a huge market out there for good quality handmade soaps.

There are two primary methods for making soap. These are:

Cold process soap-making, which involves mixing an alkali with fats or oils, and then allowing the soap to cure for several weeks

Hot process soap-making, which involves cooking the soap.

If you're willing to take the time to experiment with various soap recipes, organic ingredients, body-safe essential oils, and decorative soap molds, you could create a unique line of beautiful soaps that people will love.

Handmade soaps using organic ingredients sell very well at craft fairs, flea markets, farmer's markets, gift stores, and health food stores. You can expand your customer base by advertising your line of handmade soaps on a website or via social media.

Candle Making

Most people buy candles at some point in their lives, which has led to a boom in the popularity of specialty candles. They can be used for decorations, or to fill a room with a lovely scent as the candle burns, or for the relaxing aromatherapy effect they can give, or to create a romantic atmosphere over the dining table.

Making your own specialty homemade candles gives you the freedom to create unique designs and decorations with your products. You have the final say about which ingredients you use in your products, as well as choosing the design for any packaging you use.

You'll need to have some candle making essentials on hand before you begin, including molds, melting pot, wax, wicks, essential oils and any other ingredients you want to use.

Homemade candles sell very well at craft fairs, flea markets, farmer's markets, and gift stores. Candles are also very popular items for church or college campus fundraisers and fairs, so if you can get organizers to purchase some of your products they'll sell quickly and come back to you again to buy more stock for their next fundraising event.

You can also promote your line of candles on your website or via social media networks to let people know what you're offering and how they can order from you.

Million Dollar Case Study #4

Sandie Ledray found that many commercial brands of soap irritated her sensitive skin, so she set about finding ways to make her own soap at home. She tested and experimented with a vast range of different soap making techniques and ingredients until she found combinations that worked for her.

Ledray focused on using all-natural products that contained no animal products or animal testing. Initially, her homemade soaps were made in her kitchen and sold to friends and family.

She expanded production and decided to market her soaps to other companies as a wholesaler. Her company, Brookside Soap Inc. now creates a line of private label soap for at least six other companies, who in turn market the soaps under their own brand names.

Brookside Soap Inc. also sells its own brand-name products in health-food stores and gift shops and generates more than $200,000 a year in revenue.

Business Services

For every business idea we've discussed in this book, there is a small business owner behind it trying to keep up with the bookkeeping tasks and financial management side of their business operations.

If you have the skills and qualifications, you could easily offer your services to them. With you taking care of the mundane paperwork side of the business or the online marketing aspects, the small business owner suddenly has more free time to focus on working other facets of operations, which means generating more profits.

Bookkeeping

Being a good bookkeeper is all about understanding how a business works. If you're good at organizing financial information, your bookkeeping services could be in steady demand.

Your job will be to enter financial data into accounting software, keep track of accounts, including invoicing and receivables, tax preparation, payroll and bank reconciliation. Some business owners may also require assistance with risk management, strategic planning, and cash flow forecasting.

Contact small business owners in your local area and promote your services. Let them know you're willing to work on a contract basis, as they require the assistance, which benefits their cash flow. Offer to tailor your services to suit their specific needs.

You may need to complete a bookkeeping course at a local community college. There are also certification programs available for Quickbooks or MYOB.

Accounting

Every business owner needs access to a good accountant, especially if they hope to stay in business for any length of time.

Your job is to take care of the business's bookkeeping, invoicing, accounts, payroll and bank reconciliations. Tax planning, preparation and filing are also in-demand services for a good accountant. You may also want to offer expert assistance with risk management, business planning, strategic planning, and financial advice.

You will need to complete an accounting course and gain your certification before offering your services.

Conclusion

No matter what type of business you choose to start, the key is to always treat your fledgling enterprise as a professional business at all times. Speak to a good accountant or business consultant about the best way to structure your business to help reduce taxes and ensure you have the right type of insurance to protect you at all times.

For some types of business, you'll need to complete a DBA, or 'doing business as' application through your local county administration office to register your business name. For others, you may need to set up an LLC or a company.

You'll also need to check any state or Local County permits and licensing requirements you need to conduct your business.

Take the time to work through an appropriate bookkeeping system for your business and stay on top of your entries regularly. After all, cash flow is your business's lifeblood, so it's important that your books are kept up to date to give you a clear idea of what your finances are doing at all times.

Work on building up your business's reputation with loyal customers and consider creating a website to establish a strong online presence.

Before you know it, you could be working in a thriving business as your own boss.

Book Two

Finance: Cloud Computing, Cyber Security and Cyber Heist - Beginners Guide to Help Protect Against Online Theft in the Cyber World.

INTRODUCTION

There are a significant number of benefits to considering using cloud computing for your business needs. Yet, despite the numerous advantages, many business owners focus on the number of well-publicized security breaches and hacking attempts made on big businesses that made the switch to the cloud.

For example, large companies such as Sony Pictures, Home Depot, Target, Hilton Hotels, Ashley Madison, and Anthem had their cloud computing systems hacked in the past year or so.

When such huge corporations get hacked with relative ease, it's enough to make anyone worry about the security of cloud computing and start wondering if their sensitive business information is somehow more vulnerable.

What you may not realize is that those big companies were perhaps using cloud storage improperly.

In truth, your business's important data is only ever as vulnerable as your security protocols. The level of security on cloud-based systems is determined by two factors. The first is the amount of planning and technology used in engineering the business's security solution. The second is the business's ability to operate their computing systems securely without compromising information.

You have a huge level of control over the level of security safeguarding your sensitive business data. The key is learning ways to improve your business's operating protocols and ensure your data is always as secure as possible.

CLOUD COMPUTING, HACKERS, AND DATA SECURITY

One of the primary reasons so many hackers aim squarely at larger corporations using cloud-based computing systems is because that's where the money is. When you think about it, hackers have a job to do, just like everyone else. They have a limited amount of time in which to complete their job, so it makes sense to invest their time and efforts into businesses that are likely to give them the best possible results. For this reason, hackers see large businesses using improperly secured cloud-based computing systems as being somewhat of a jackpot.

When you take all this into consideration, it suddenly appears as though the number of cyber-attacks against cloud-based systems has increased.

What many of those media reports fail to mention is that the sheer number of companies that have switched to a cloud environment has also increased. With more companies moving to the cloud and away from in-house data storage solutions and servers, of course it seems as though just those with cloud-based services are being targeted.

Most of those organizations are shifting their services and data into the cloud to take advantage of the increased flexibility, potential cost-savings, and the ability to scale services when they're required.

Unfortunately, far too many businesses rely on 'standard' cloud installation processes, instead of customizing their cloud computing solutions and security settings to their own individual needs. A standard installation can be replicated across lots of different enterprises and companies, which mean all the security settings are similar – and therefore become more vulnerable to cyber-attack.

Think about it this way: a thief could break into your home and steal your personal belongings. However, that same thief could also take a bigger risk by breaking into a bank and get a much bigger payoff. The bank has significantly more security in place than your personal home, but the bigger payoff is worth the risk to some thieves.

Now translate that same analogy into cloud computing. Hackers aim at larger cloud servers because that's where the bigger payoff is for them. Imagine a hacker breaking into a massive cloud database such as Gmail and grabbing data from millions of email accounts.

However, there will always be some hackers who aim at the easy targets, which include those companies with poorly secured in-house servers and data systems. The payoff might be smaller, but the work is much easier for them to get in and get back out again with your sensitive data. When you boil it down, a cloud-based system is inherently more secure overall, as a larger cloud service provider such as Google or Amazon or Microsoft needs to focus strongly on being as secure as possible to reduce the threat of cyber-attack on millions of accounts.

In reality, hackers still target onsite data servers at the same frequency as they always did. It's merely the number of businesses that have moved to cloud services that has increased, which shows up on statistics as a sharp increase in cloud-based cyber-attacks.

Cyber-Crime Activities in the Cloud

The key factor in keeping cloud-based applications secure and reduce the risk of cyber-attack is to understand that security in the cloud should be a shared responsibility. The cloud provider needs to focus on ensuring that security strategies are as stringent as possible.
However, it's equally up to you as the customer to ensure that you understand what security measures you need to worry about to secure your data.
Some examples of the type of cyber-crime activities that cloud service providers face on a daily basis include:

Authentication Issues

Unauthorized access to systems can occur when someone username and password combination has been gained without the person's authorization.

Passwords can be obtained by people responding to phishing emails, or fake emails claiming to be from legitimate service providers asking the user to log into a false account.

Passwords can also be gained using key-logging software or hacked using brute force.

One of the easiest ways hackers gain access to cloud-based servers is by guessing people's password. A simple password using a pet's name or child's name is always easy for a hacker to work out, especially if those names are publicly available on social media accounts. Likewise, choosing easy answers to secret questions where the answers are publicly available just makes a hacker's job easier.

Denial of Service Attacks

A Denial of Service (DoS) attack against a cloud service provider can leave users with no access to their accounts. DoS attacks occur by the attacker sending a flood of traffic to a website or group or websites on a host's server designed to overwhelm the servers and make them inaccessible.

Attacks can be launched using a 'botnet', which is a network of machines that distribute the source of the attack and make it more difficult to track its origins. A distributed denial of service attack is known as a DDoS.

Cloud Computing for Criminal Activities

Some cyber-criminals will use cloud-computing accounts to create new accounts used specifically for criminal purposes. Such accounts can be controlled using a botnet, which is then used to command and control a DDoS attack, or to launch a cyber-attack to overcome password restrictions on the cloud service provider's servers.

It's possible for criminals to create new cloud computing accounts using stolen credentials and stolen credit card details, which makes it even more difficult to track the origin of the attack.

Malware

While a cloud service provider's servers may be heavily monitored and updated with anti-virus and malware scanning capabilities, it is still possible for their servers to become vulnerable to infection.

For example, if one user's website is compromised with malware it's possible for the cloud provider's servers to become infected too, spreading to the virtual machines of multiple other clients.

Network or Packet Sniffing

Network or packet sniffing is all about the hacker intercepting network traffic. Any data that is transmitted across a network, including passwords, can be captured and read if they're not properly encrypted. In a cloud-computing environment, it's especially important to encrypt passwords and authentication codes properly, as they play an integral role in how the user accesses the cloud provider's services.

Access Management Issues

It's unfortunately common for many businesses to fail to restrict employee's access to cloud computing services once they leave their job. Once that employee leaves the organization, any passwords or other access information they have can allow them to compromise the business's data.

Former employees have been known to steal information, copy it, delete it, or otherwise alter it. For some, the intention behind the attack may be purely malicious, but for others it may be for the purpose of creating a competing business.

Physical Attacks on Servers

The servers provided by cloud service providers still need a physical home. Enormous data centers with intricate security systems in place usually house endless rows of physical servers that store every user's data.

While it's not common, it is possible for those servers and the data center to be physically attacked. In 2011, two people attacked a data center in Chicago, taking an employee hostage before using that employee's security pass and fingerprints to gain access to the center.

When you consider the sheer number of threats faced by cloud-based computing services, it's no wonder they're so vigilant about their security measures. They provide as much security surrounding protection of user data as possible, which makes them a significantly safer environment than an in-house data storage network system.

What they can't control is how their users treat their own personal security. That's up to you.

The Dark Web - Silk Road

The Dark Web is the shady underworld of the Internet. It's the place where hackers, cyber-criminals, and identity thieves thrive, and it bears very little resemblance to the Internet landscape you thought you knew. There's also a separate online realm, known as the Deep Web. Before you can get some idea about the size and extent of the Dark Web and Deep Web, it might be important to draw an analogy.

Surface Web

Imagine the size and scope of the Internet, as you know it. All the search engines and social media sites and business websites and game sites you can access on a regular basis. Even some of those shady sites and online gambling sites sit on this level, especially if you found them on a random Google search.
These sites all form the Internet, as the majority of people understand it.
It's estimated that the public face of the Internet encompasses around **4%** of all the www content you see.

Deep Web

Now, imagine all those things are just the little tip of the iceberg showing above the surface. What lurks just below the surface is known as the Deep Web, or sometimes also called the

Dark Net, and it's approximately **500 times** the size of the surface web.

Before you start thinking everything down in the Deep Web is illegal, immoral, sinister, or otherwise sleazy, consider some of the completely legal things hidden in obscurity down here:

1st Layer of the Deep Web

The first layer of the Deep Web is littered with web services and databases that conventional search engines can't index, such as Government databases and archived inner pages of private websites. These are completely legal. They're just inaccessible to the general public. Think of sites like members-only websites or password-protected content.

Even your Facebook newsfeed is down here on the first layer of the Deep Web, simply because it can't be indexed by the search engines. Incidentally, this first layer is where most of your encrypted and unindexed data sits in the cloud.

2nd Layer of the Deep Web: The Dark Web

Sink a little deeper into the depths and you'll find the next layer of the Deep Web, known as the Dark Web. This is the dark side of the Internet people think of when they picture shady underworld dealings and illegal activities. The Dark Net is where most of the illegal, notorious, criminal, and downright sleazy side of the underworld thrives.

The Dark Net is the realm where those torrent-sharing sites, pirated software, pirated movie sites, and illegal download sites exist. It's where those highly illegal sites hide. It's where the database for the Hidden WikiLeaks hides.
There are also sections that focus on illegal gambling, selling guns, trafficking drugs, and offers of contract murder, among plenty of other things. Hackers and cyber-thieves also thrive down here.
It's also the domain of the Silk Road. We'll go into Silk Road and the Dark Web in some more detail a bit later in this chapter.

3rd Layer of the Deep Web

The third layer of the Deep Web is where the vast majority of deep traffic flows, and most of it is completely legal. It's also the layer that cyber-thieves find the most interesting.

This is where the corporate and government traffic lives on alternate, internal, and private networks, like LANs, WANs, and PANs. For example, your online bank account page is down here. The page where you type in your credit card information to complete an online purchase is down here.

It's hidden from the public level of the Internet because of its sensitive nature, which means it's delegated to limited-access only down in the Deep Web. And it's all totally legal.

Of course, some of the sensitive and private data stored in the cloud is also hidden down here in the 3rd layer of the Deep Web.

Unfortunately, this is the area hackers and cyber-thieves want to access to find their jackpots of sensitive data and private information. It's here where you need to be most vigilant about your organization's cyber-security.

The Silk Road

The Silk Road was an enormous black marketplace hidden in the depths of the Dark Web. It was best known as a platform for selling illegal drugs until the FBI seized it in October 2013. It didn't take long for The Silk Road 2.0 to emerge in its place and continue the thriving underworld business. Of course, that was also seized during a bust by the feds in November 2014.

The Diabolus Market was hastily renamed to Silk Road 3 Reloaded. Now The Silk Road 3.0 is up and active with support from multiple different cryptocurrencies, along with a range of other Dark Net underworld drug markets, including Green Road, Onion Pharma, Agora, and TheRealDeal.

Other dark marketplaces are designed to sell illegal drugs, weapons, guns, ammunition, hitmen for hire, assassinations, and a range of other sinister and illicit services.

Hackers thrive on the Silk Road, among other places on the Dark Web, as they're able to sell their hacking services to whoever wants them. For example, a listing found on Tor's Hidden Links directory for hidden Dark Web services has the following listing for a hacker's services for sale:

Rent-A-Hacker – Hacking, DDoS, Social Engineering, Espionage, Ruining People

Hackers and cyber-thieves are able to sell stolen information on the Dark Web, such as stolen identities, stolen Social Security numbers, fake

IDs and driver's licenses, and stolen credit card information.

Cyber-thieves also use the Silk Road to sell skimmed credit card information, or to create brand new identities for people. There are multiple sites listed on Tor's Hidden Links directory for providing other forms of identification.

Tor's Hidden Links directory also lists a huge number of financial services available, including money laundering, high quality counterfeit money for sale, skimmed and stolen credit cards, and stolen login details for live bank accounts with actual US dollar balances in them.

Dark Web

The illegal side of the Deep Web is that area that is only accessible via the heavily encrypted network through a specialized routing protocol. This area is known as the Dark Web.

The Dark Web is the access via the encrypted network that is only accessible using a routing protocol such as The Onion Router, or TOR network.

The Onion Router (Tor) is an anonymous browsing client that uses the Tor Hidden Service Protocol to access sites on the Deep Web and the Dark Web.

The Tor network was created by the US Naval Research Laboratory for the purposes of creating a secure avenue for government communications. Since that time the network has entered the public domain.

The Tor browser can be downloaded for free and it's completely legal, as it's designed to keep the user's personal information secret. It's actually a nifty way to protect Internet users from identity theft. Some people use it to keep their kids safe on the Internet. Even law enforcement agencies use the Tor network for their anonymous tip lines and whistleblowing sites.

Users lurking in the underworld of the Dark Web don't access their version of the Internet straight through their computer. Rather, some will access the net using their Tor browser. Some will also use proxy servers, or a deeply layered structure of servers to route their traffic before it even reaches the anonymous Tor network. They also take particular care with their personal computer security settings to minimize the potential risks. If you're not careful when playing around in this realm, you can expect a visit from the FBI in due course.

The Dark Web has a number of hidden and anonymous email services and messaging services that allow people to communicate without revealing anything about their location or identity. There are anonymous forums and chatboards and several social networks, including the real Facebook's alternative .onion domain. Of course, regulars on the Dark Web tend to prefer BlackBook as their Dark Web social network of choice.

Website links on the Dark Web don't look much like the regular www hyperlinks the vast majority of people use on the Surface Web every day. Instead, links down in the Dark Web look more like this:

http://hos8et4ng6iar5zo7c.onion/

The sites on the Dark Web aren't indexed anywhere, so it's up to the individual site owners to list their .onion domains on a directory site such as Tor's Hidden Links. The Tor Hidden Links directory displays the number of sites hiding on the Dark Web at around 30,000, which is about 0.03% of the total data and information online. Of course, that's just the number of sites that are voluntarily added to the directory.

By comparison, the public face of the Internet encompasses around 4% of the WWW content online and there are now more than a billion indexed websites.

There are also a massive number of unknown or unindexed sites lurking in the shadows that are only available to those who have access to the private link directly. Not everyone with a site on the Dark Web wants their link shared, displayed or made available. After all, many people are there to maintain their anonymity.

The remaining amount of information hiding on the Deep Web is simply private information that isn't indexed on search engines from government organizations, corporate networks, banks, and other private sites.

Bitcoins: Dark Web Currency

Anyone who is unfamiliar with the Dark Web may wonder why transactions aren't traced or tracked through bank accounts and deposits by Interpol or various other cyber-crime law enforcement departments.

That's because the vast majority of transactions on the Dark Web marketplaces are conducted using Bitcoins, which is a digital cryptocurrency that gives the user a certain amount of anonymity. Bitcoin is a decentralized and unregulated type of currency that is free of the reins of any one government agency. As it's not backed by any government, the value of Bitcoin can fluctuate from day to day.

The user purchases Bitcoins, which are a completely legal currency and legitimate digital currency, and places them into their Bitcoin wallet. The buyer then transfers their Bitcoins into an anonymous wallet, where all of the

Bitcoins are mixed with other Bitcoins that have been deposited by other users, so the flow of Bitcoins becomes untraceable.

Some marketplaces and commerce sites on the Dark Web use an escrow system to complete transactions. The buyer purchases items from the seller and pays for that transaction using the mixed Bitcoins in the anonymous wallet.

Sellers can exchange the Bitcoins they received for selling their products or services for real cash. Of course, there are multiple money laundering (and Bitcoin laundering) services available on the Dark Web, along with the ease of mixing Bitcoins in an anonymous wallet before withdrawing them anywhere, so there's very little trace of where they came from and who they're going to.

GLOBAL CYBER-THEFT AND COMPUTER FORENSICS

International cybercrime and global cyber-theft are a major challenge for law enforcement agencies, as the laws in many countries aren't geared up to deal with online crime. In fact, it's common for many criminals to conduct their crimes over the Internet as a way to take advantage of the less severe punishments.
As a result, computer forensics is used to find evidence on computers and other forms of digital storage media. Computer forensics is a branch of digital forensic science that is most commonly associated with the investigation of cybercrime. Evidence recovered during an authentic computer forensics audit may be used as reliable evidence in U.S. and European court proceedings.

Believe it or not, one of the oldest methods for catching cyber-criminals is still the most effective for catching cyber-criminals. Undercover cybercrime law enforcement officers are responsible for a large number of busts and heists of Dark Web marketplaces in recent years.

Yet, the Dark Web and hackers aren't solely responsible for all of the global cybercrime problems. There is a broad range of cybercrimes that are investigated by computer forensics teams.

These include:

Hacking: accessing a computer system illegally.

Cyber-Attacks: denial of service (DoS) and distributed denial of service (DDoS) attacks designed to make a network unavailable to its intended users.

Phishing scams: fraudsters send out emails that sometimes look like official communications from banks, asking customers to verify their log in details and passwords.

Data Espionage: intercepting traffic and communications between users, including emails, chat conversations, or VoIP communications. This type of crime may also be called session hijacking or session riding.

Identity Theft: stealing private information, including login and password details, passport numbers, date of birth, Social Security numbers and other identifying details.

Malware: Malicious software, or malware, is designed to disrupt computer options, gather sensitive information, or to gain access to private computer systems. Access to a business's cloud computing account may be achieved if the device accessing the cloud service is compromised.

Keyloggers: Keystroke logging malware records the keys struck on a keyboard without the user being aware that their actions are being monitored. The intention is to capture the user's login and password details.

Cyber-Forgery: manipulating or falsifying digital documents.

Cyber-Fraud: cyber-fraud offenses include credit card fraud, Internet banking fraud and online auction fraud.

Social Engineering: a social engineering scam refers to a type of intrusion that fools the victim into downloading malware or giving out personal information. It's often used in emails or social networking chats and is effective for attacking well-protected computer systems.

Copyright Offenses: distribution of illegally pirated software, movies, music, or books.

Trademark Violations: cybersquatting is the act of using an Internet domain name with the intention of profiting from the use of a trademarked name belonging to someone else. The cybersquatter will then offer to sell the domain to the company that owns the trademark at an inflated price.

Cyber-terrorism: spreading propaganda, gathering information, publishing training material, financing terrorist organizations, or preparing for real-world attacks.

Cyber-Laundering: conducting crimes through the use of virtual currencies or via cryptocurrencies. This section of cybercrime also includes people laundering cash by using online gaming, through digital cryptocurrencies, or using micro-payments.

With so many different cyber-crime activities to watch for, protecting your security and preventing an attack can seem daunting.

Fortunately, there are some things everyone can do to reduce the risk of becoming the target of a cyber-attack.

PREVENTION FOR YOUR   ORGANIZATION

Knowing that there are hackers and cyber-thieves lurking on the Dark Web should give you some incentive to review your organization's security settings.

However, did you know that a large percentage of security breaches and data leaks come from within the organization itself? Many employees may not even realize they could be compromising the company's computer security with their actions, simply due to lack of training. Many organizations may also be compromised by outdated anti-virus software and a lack of proper security implementation.

No matter whether your computing systems are on an in-house network server or hosted in the cloud, here are some things you can do to prevent a cyber-attack for your organization:

Check Current Cyber Health

It's important to check what the current health status of your computing systems looks like before you start updating or upgrading anything. Hire an IT security consultant to give you a complete overview of your cyber health needs to ensure nothing is overlooked and have a PEN

(Penetration) Test performed on your network to see how well it might withstand a cyber-attack.

Implement Security Measures

Be sure your company's anti-virus software is up to date across all of your computer terminals and any tablet PCs or other mobile devices that connect to the organization's network. Back up all company data regularly and ensure backup copies are stored securely.
Secure internal network servers and connections, and verify the security settings of any cloud-based services you use.
Consider adding an extra layer of protection with Multifactor Authentication (MFA). This is a type of security system that requires more than one method of authentication to verify the user's identity that can be invaluable for protecting the

identities of users at the same time as securing access to corporate networks.

Protect Against Malicious Attacks

Protect your organization from malicious traffic attacks with DDoS (Distributed Denial of Service) protection. There are three primary types of DDoS attacks that could cripple a server, network or corporate infrastructure. **These are:**

- **Volume-based attacks**: a swarm of requests, usually showing illegitimate IP addresses, intended to overwhelm site bandwidth with a flood of traffic.
- **Protocol attacks**: sending open requests (TCP/IP requests) with fake IPs in an effort

to drain resources so they're unable to answer legitimate requests, making the system unavailable for legitimate users.

- **Application layer attacks**: also called Layer 7 attacks, these are slow and stealthy attacks that send seemingly harmless requests intended to bring down a web server.

You can fortify against malicious traffic attacks by ensuring that servers are patched promptly. Use a small backup circuit and segregate any key servers. Then test your anti-DoS service to be sure key employees or consultants know what to do in case of an attack.

There are many security solutions available that offer excellent DDoS protection services. Be sure your investment in any DDoS protection is in proportion with the actual business risk, but also ensure that your protection maintenance can be scaled as your business needs evolve.

Web App Attacks

If your organization uses online payment processing facilities or online point-of-sale (POS) software, it's important to protect against web app attacks and POS intrusions. Businesses in the retail, information, hospitality, and manufacturing industries are particularly at risk here.

You can help to prevent misuse of stolen information or exploitation of vulnerabilities by using two-factor authentication for transactions. Consider switching your current web apps to a static content-management system. Set your web apps to lock accounts after a specified number of failed login attempts, and ensure that you monitor any outbound connections.

To reduce the risk of POS intrusions, limit any remote access to your POS systems by third-party companies and enforce strong password policies. Ideally, POS systems should use two-factor authentication.

Create Cyber-Security Policies

Create some clearly-worded cyber-security policies and train all company employees on IT risk. Determine precisely what your expectations are in terms of cyber-security and document it. Include a 'safe-use' flash drive policy for all employees to reduce the risk of a compromised flash drive being used in your business systems.

Review all company user accounts and remove access to any former employees, if this hasn't been done already. Set up control systems to watch for data transfers out of the organization to protect against data theft from inside the company.

Train Employees on Cyber-Security Policies

Invest the time and effort to train every employee within the organization on your company's cyber-security policies. It's important that every person within your business understands the importance of acting responsibly with company assets and data.

All staff members also need to understand their roles and your expectations of any internet and intranet usage during working hours, including accessing personal emails and social media on company devices and connecting unsecured mobile devices to local Wi-Fi networks.

Prevention for the Home User

While ensuring that all company and business IT systems are secured, it's also important to protect home computers and personal devices against cyber-attack.
Here are some simple steps you can take to reduce the risk of a cyber-attack on personal systems:

Home Computing Systems

- Keep all of your operating systems (OS), Antivirus, antispyware, and other software up-to-date
- Enable your firewall
- Secure your wireless network with WPA encryption and set a strong password

- Install any security updates or patches for your operating system promptly
- Make sure your home wireless network is secure
- Never download or install unfamiliar programs onto your system
- Don't insert untrusted thumb drives or data storage drives into your computer

Passwords

- Create secure passwords for any online accounts that contain a combination of upper- and lower-case letters, numbers and symbols
- Don't use publicly-available names or phrases in your password (such as pet's or kid's names)
- Don't use the same password for multiple services
- Change passwords regularly

- If necessary, use a password management service to keep track of different passwords for various services
- Don't use the option for your operating system to automatically remember your passwords
- Never give out your passwords to anyone

File Usage and Access

- Encrypt your files
- Disable file sharing on your computer
- Delete any cookies saved on your computer
- Delete your internet browsing history regularly

Online Activity

- Always log on directly to business website. Don't click through to the website from an email link

- Make sure a website is secure before you enter any personal information: i.e. make sure the web address starts with the prefix https://
- Think before you click: Be extra careful while downloading random free applications
- Never use public Wi-Fi for financial transactions. Only use trusted private computers or devices to keep your information secure.
- Set your Internet browser to block pop-up ads. Some unscrupulous people use pop-up ads to install malicious software on your computer.
- Be vigilant about phishing websites that look like legitimate business sites, but are really fake sites seeking your personal information. Avoid any site asking for personal information that could compromise your online identity.

Email Usage

- Change your email settings so that attachments aren't automatically downloaded
- Never click on links in emails, even if you think the email appears legitimate. If you hover your mouse over the link in an email you can often see the website address under the visible link may be very different to the anchor-text written there for you to see.
- Type website addresses into your browser directly to ensure you are taken to the correct site, instead of a malicious site.
- Never open attachments in emails. Set your email settings so you don't' automatically download attachments.
- Never give out personal information in an email, such as passwords, credit card numbers or bank account details

Social Media

Be careful about how much information you give out on social media. It's surprising how much information people can gather about you without your knowledge just with simple social media updates.

- Your kid's names and pet's names are often publicly available just by chatting about them or posting pics of them.
- If you complain about the service at your bank on social media, a hacker now has that information about what company you do your banking with, making you an easy target for identity theft.
- If you post photos of your home or your car, blur out the house number or license plates, as these things also give away a lot about your identity to unscrupulous people.
- Don't answer silly questions on social media that ask you to enter your full name and date

of birth to see a cool pic pop up when you're done.

Smartphone Security

Most people are aware of the importance of protecting their home computer systems, but they don't always consider doing the same thing with mobile devices.

The number of people accessing the Internet and using mobile apps is increasing daily. Of course, many smartphones are prone to viruses, malware, keyloggers and theft.

If your cell phone was stolen by an unscrupulous person, it's likely the thief would have access to your online banking details, complete with passwords and PINs, your emails, your social media accounts, passwords to your home Wi-Fi connection, and a range of other personal information.

You can protect your smartphone by doing the following:

- Set a pin code or password on your lock screen. It provides an extra layer of difficulty for a thief trying to access your phone
- Install and enable remote services, such as setting a remote lock, remote wipe, and GPS location for tracking a lost or stolen phone
- Back up your data regularly by copying documents, pictures and other data to your computer.
- Use encryption where you can. Not every smartphone operating system offers this option, but if you can you should encrypt your data, including the external memory card, or SD card.
- Use smartphone antivirus software to reduce the risk of infection with malware or viruses

- Don't connect to untrusted Wi-Fi access
  points. Many public Wi-Fi points, such as
  airports, coffee shops, or fast-food
  restaurants may have compromised
  connectivity.
- Always enable operating system updates and
  app updates promptly to reduce the risk of
  being exposed to attack

Monitor your Credit Report File Regularly
A big part of being vigilant about identity theft
is making sure someone doesn't already have
your information and is using it for their own
gain – and to your detriment. The sooner you
catch any suspicious activity, the easier it is to
stop it.
Order a copy of your credit report file regularly
and review it carefully for any transactions or
entries that don't look familiar.

Protect Physical Documentation

Identity theft isn't limited to just your online activities. It's also important you protect your identity on any physically printed documentation.

Paper documents, such as bank statements, utility bills, tax returns, and driving license information should be filed securely. Always shred any documents you do not need, especially if they contain your personal information.

Protect Your Children Online

Anyone with kids who use the Internet faces a bit of a challenge. On the one hand, it's important for kids to experience new technologies. On the other hand, there are plenty of inherent dangers for kids online.

Fortunately, there is security software available that can help to restrict the amount of things kids are able to see and do online. Perhaps the biggest issue parents face is having their child preyed upon by a predator online. Using specific software can help to filter the types of sites kids are able to surf.

Despite the ability to restrict the type of content they can view, kids can also unknowingly compromise your family's privacy and identity. It's important that children are taught how important it is to protect their personal information. Many child-oriented websites focus on obtaining information from kids by asking them to fill in surveys or forms in exchange for a prize. What kids may not realize is that they give out a lot of personal information when registering for these things, including their gender, age, and favorite place to hang out.

Social media sites and chat rooms also pose numerous dangers to kids. Ensure your kids understand the basic rules for using any social networking sites, including protecting their passwords and being careful about posting identifying information.

Teach kids not to download games or apps from unfamiliar or untrusted sources. Some parents allow kids to download music, games and apps that may require credit card information, so ensure that they're monitored when making purchases. Never allow kids to enter your credit card details into an unsecured website.

Kids can explore, learn and enjoy their online interest safely, but there are some simple steps every parent can take to protect them from online threats and inappropriate content.

Conclusion

Protecting your family against cybercrime doesn't need to be a daunting task. In fact, as long as you remain vigilant about your personal information and take appropriate steps to protect yourself, you should never experience any major problems.

Of course, if you own a business or company, your livelihood could be severely affected if your organization becomes the target of a cyber-attack from someone with malicious intent. Implement strong cyber-security strategies and work closely with an IT security consultant to ensure your business computing systems are protected at all times.

As long as you stay on top of your security needs, you'll be taking positive steps to reduce the risk of ever becoming a target of cyber-attack or cyber-theft.

Other Available Books:

Money: Think Outside the Cube: 2-Book Money Making Boxed Set Bundle Strategies

In The Pursuit of Wisdom: The Principal Thing

Investing in Gold and Silver Bullion - The
Ultimate Safe Haven Investments

Nigerian Stock Market Investment: 2 Books
with Bonus Content

The Dividend Millionaire: Investing for Income
and Winning in the Stock Market

Economic Crisis: Surviving Global Currency
Collapse - Safeguard Your Financial Future
with Silver and Gold

Passionate about Stock Investing: The Quick
Guide to Investing in the Stock Market

Guide to Investing in the Nigerian Stock Market

Building Wealth with Dividend Stocks in the
Nigerian Stock Market (Dividends - Stocks
Secret Weapon)

Beginners Basic Guide to Investing in Gold and Silver Boxed Set

Precious Metals Investing For Beginners: The Quick Guide to Platinum and Palladium

Bitcoin and Digital Currency for Beginners: The Basic Little Guide

Child Millionaire: Stock Market Investing for Beginners - How to Build Wealth the Smart Way for Your Child

Christian Living: 2 Books with Bonus Content

Beginners Quick Guide to Passive Income: Learn Proven Ways to Earn Extra Income in the Cyber World

Taming the Tongue: The Power of Spoken Words

The Power of Positive Affirmations: Each Day a
New Beginning

The Real Estate Millionaire: Beginners Quick
Start Guide to Investing In Properties.

Business: How to Quickly Make Real Money -
Effective Methods to Make More Money

Business and Money: 4-Book Complete
Collection Boxed Set For Beginners

If you would like to share this book with another person, please purchase an additional copy for each recipient. Thank you for respecting the hard work of this author. Thank you for your support